J
C

by Brian Platt

Whatever they put in that Cat food ... I like it!
Brian Platt

Published by Accent Press Ltd – 2005
www.accentpress.co.uk
ISBN 0954867335
Copyright © Brian Platt - 2005
The rights of Brian Platt have been asserted.

All rights reserved. No part of this book may be reproduced, stored in a retrieval system, or transmitted in any form or by any means, electronic, electrostatic, magnetic tape, mechanical, photocopying, recording or otherwise, without written permission from the publishers: Accent Press Ltd, PO Box 50, Pembroke Dock, Pembrokeshire SA72 6WY.

Printed and bound in China

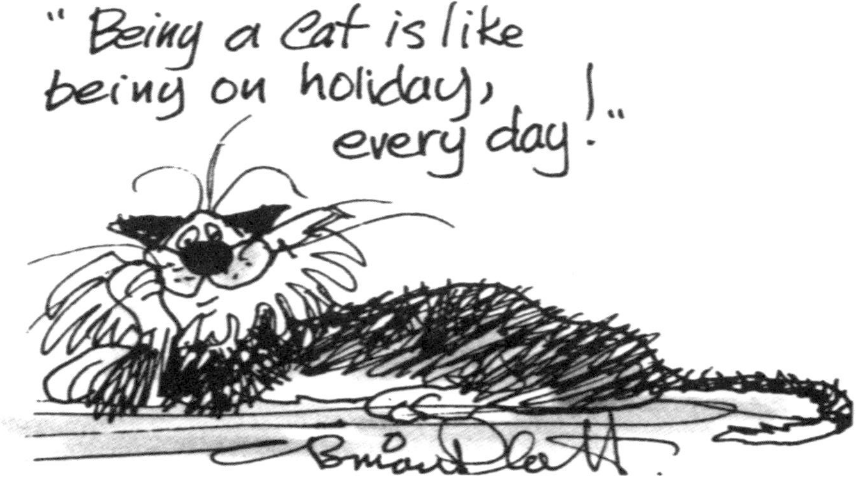
" Being a Cat is like
being on holiday,
every day!"

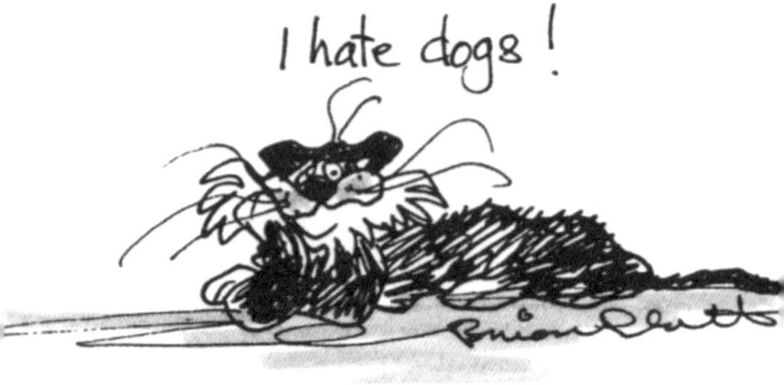
I hate dogs!

Nobody naps like a cat!

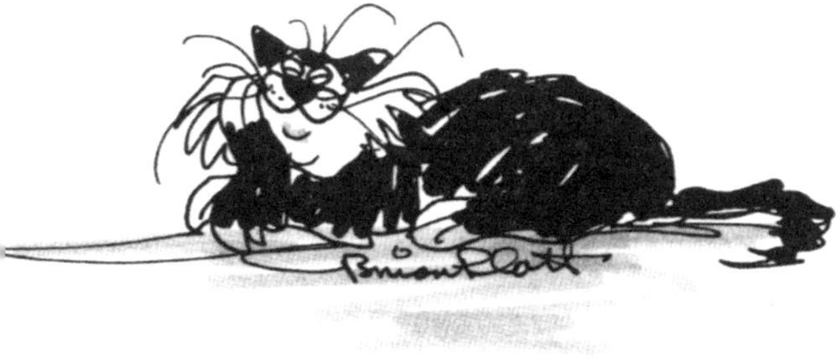

... even cat's get old !

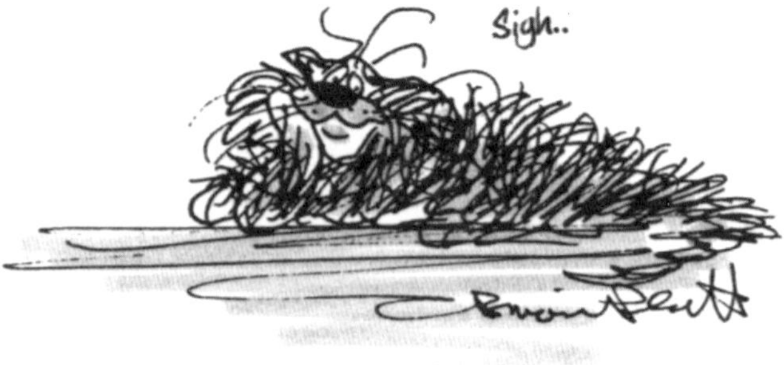
Sigh..

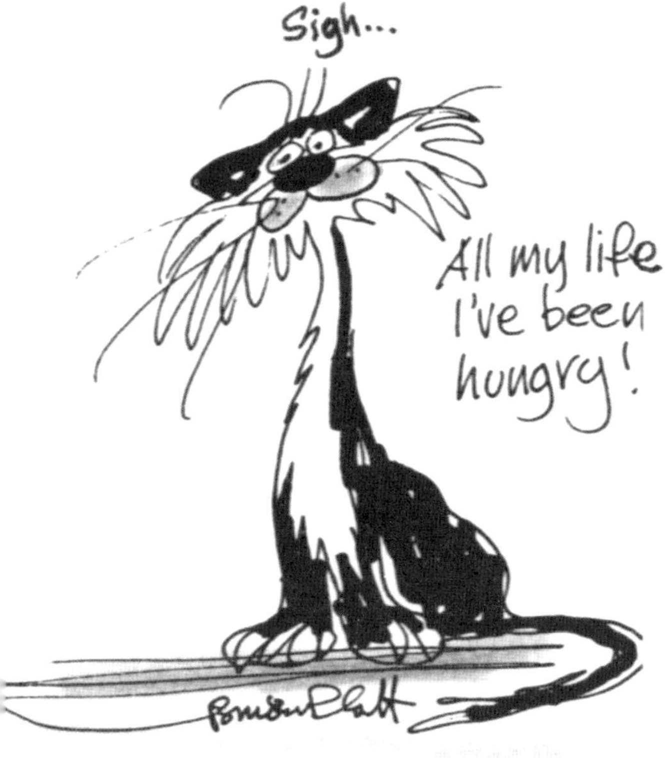
Sigh...
All my life I've been hungry!

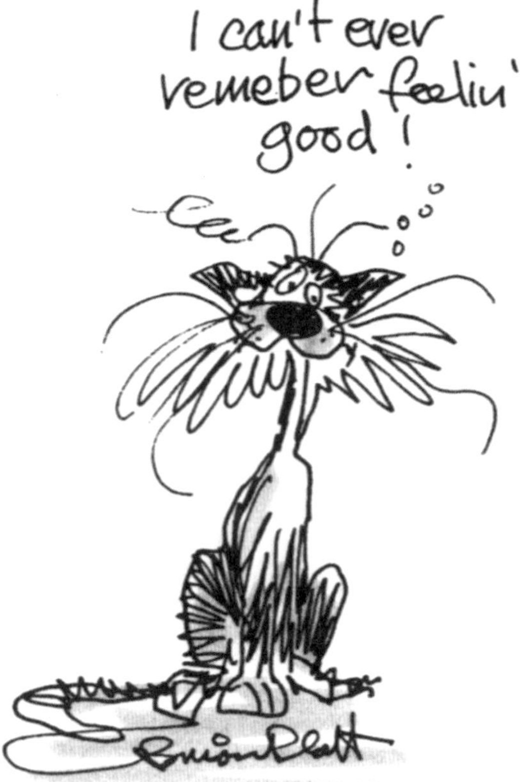
I can't ever remeber feelin' good!

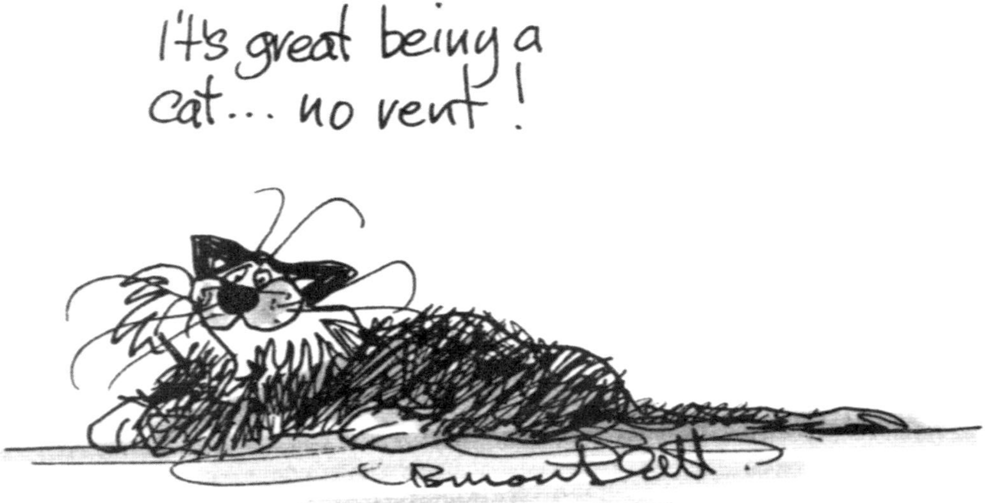
It's great being a cat... no rent!

It's my birthday today... I wonder if i'll get a FISH CAKE?

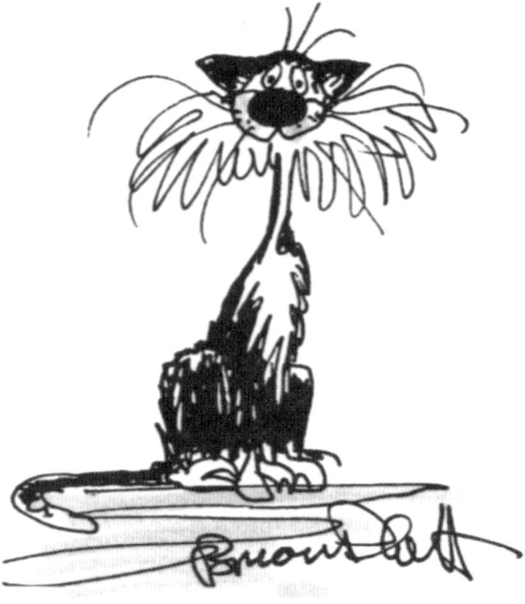

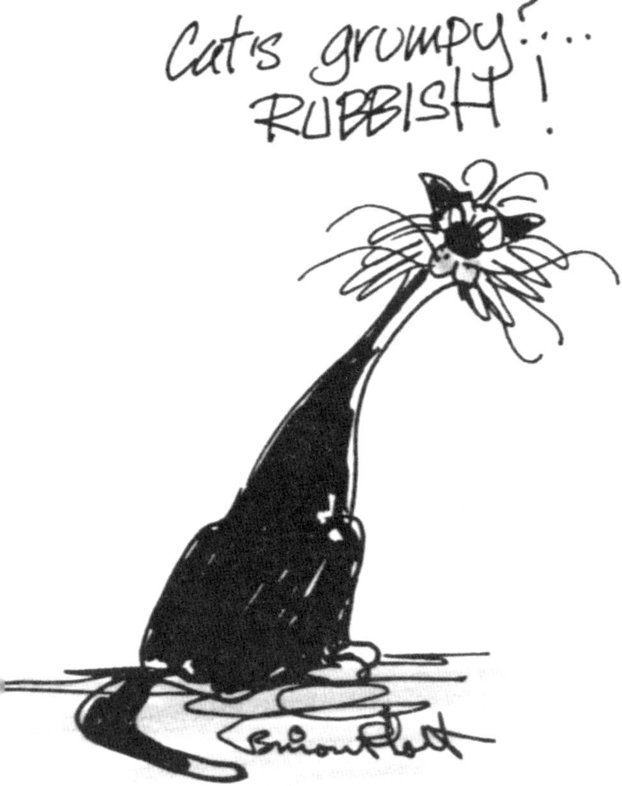
Cat's grumpy?...
RUBBISH!

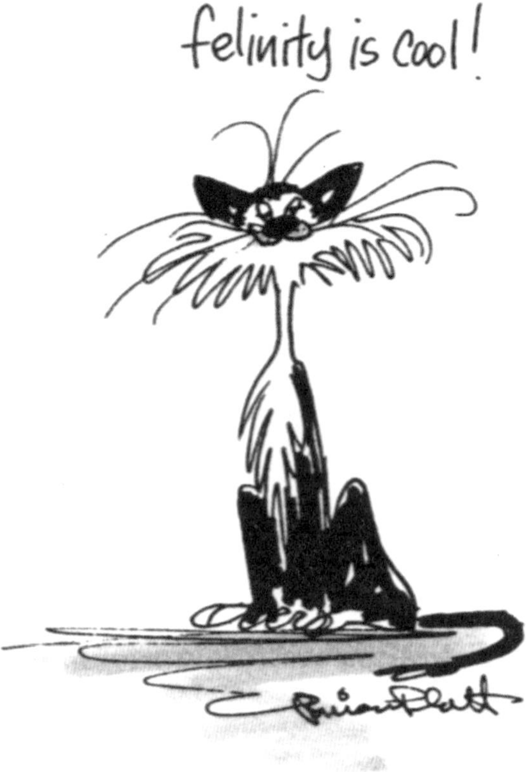
felinity is cool!

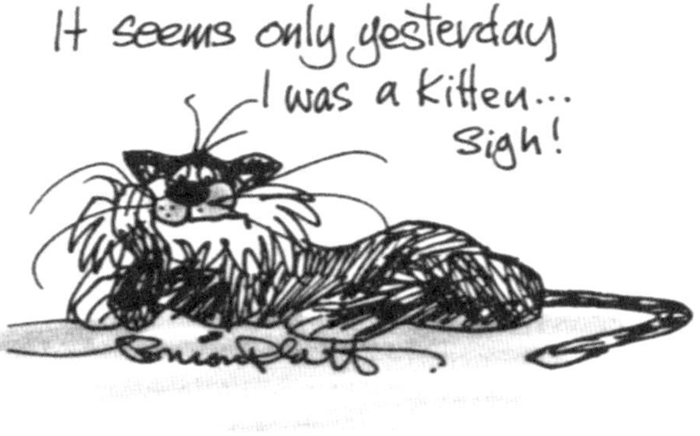
It seems only yesterday
I was a kitten...
sigh!

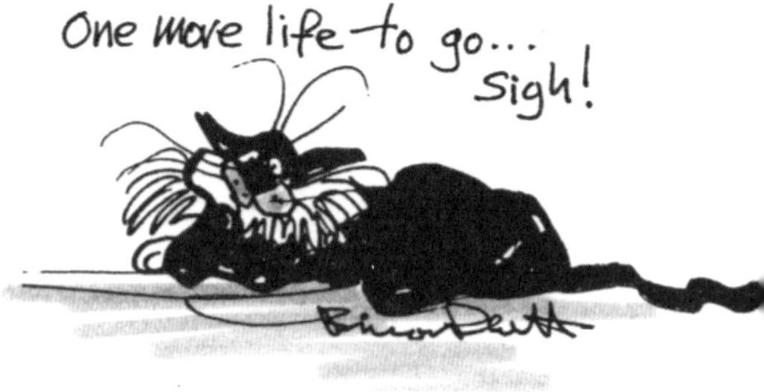
One more life to go... sigh!

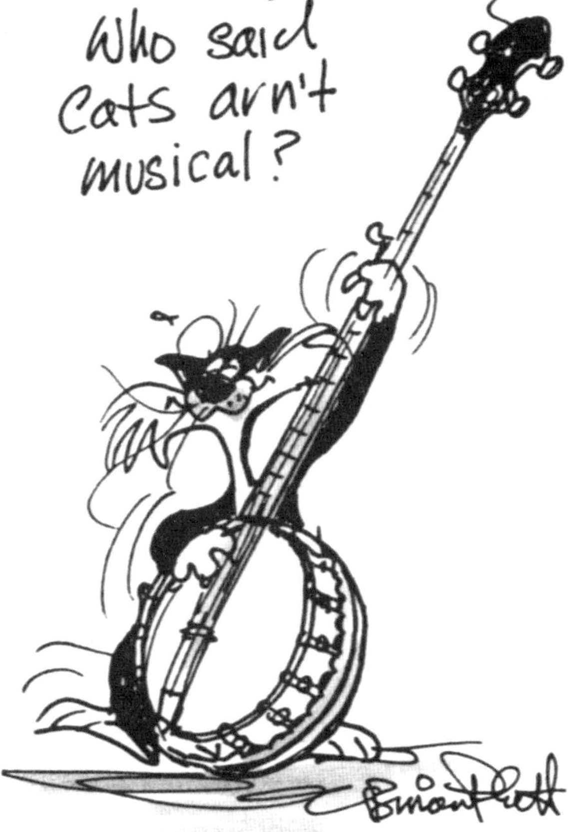
Who said
Cats arn't
musical?

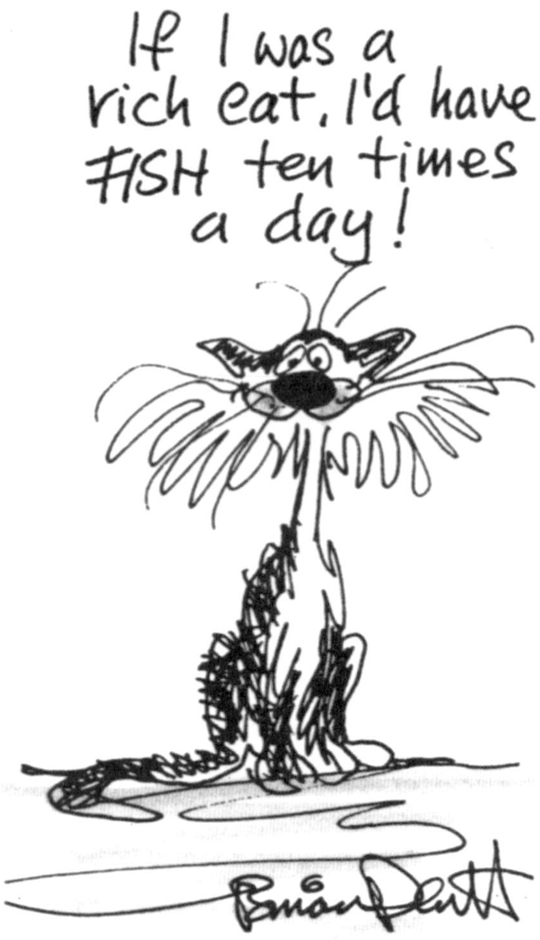
If I was a rich cat, I'd have FISH ten times a day!

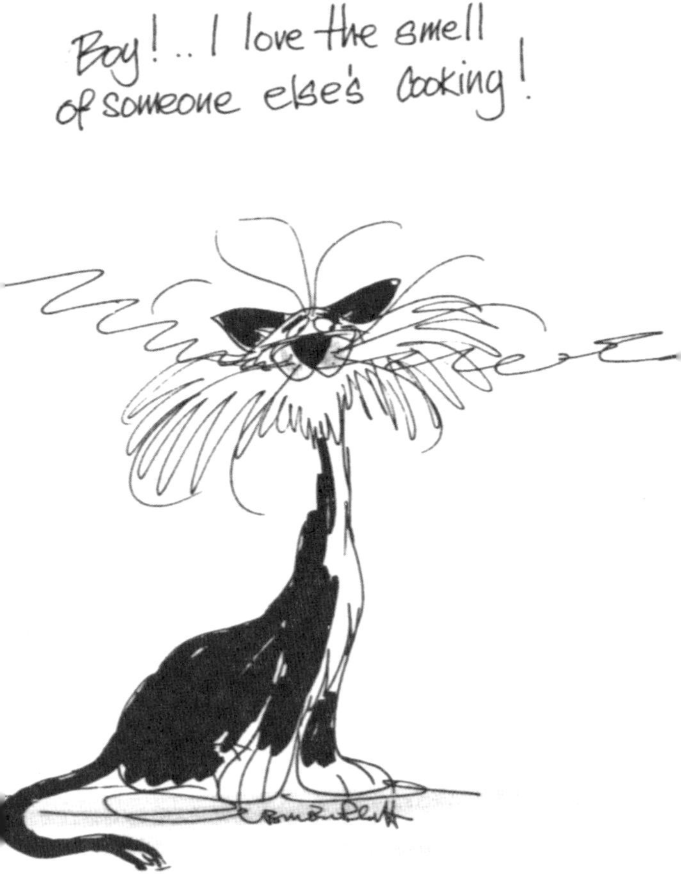
Boy! .. I love the smell
of someone else's cooking!

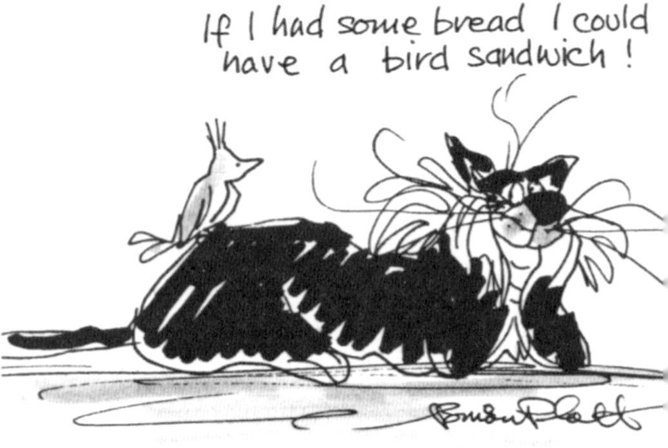
If I had some bread I could have a bird sandwich!

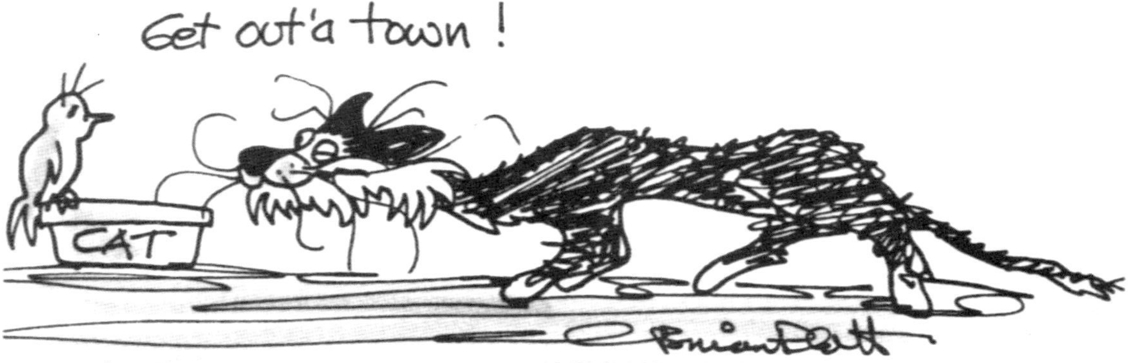
Get out'a town !
CAT

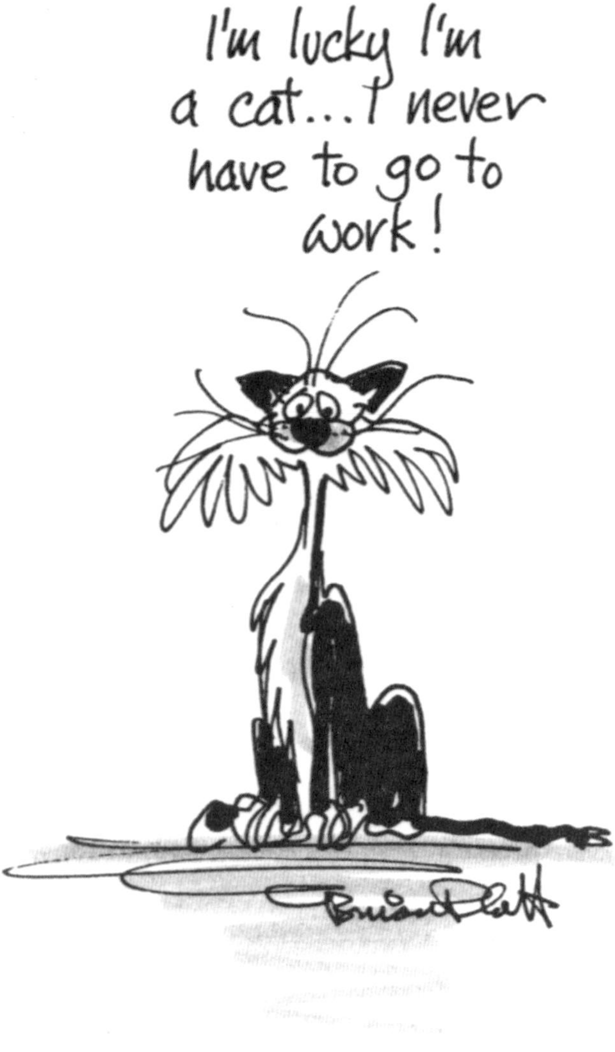
I'm lucky I'm a cat... I never have to go to work!

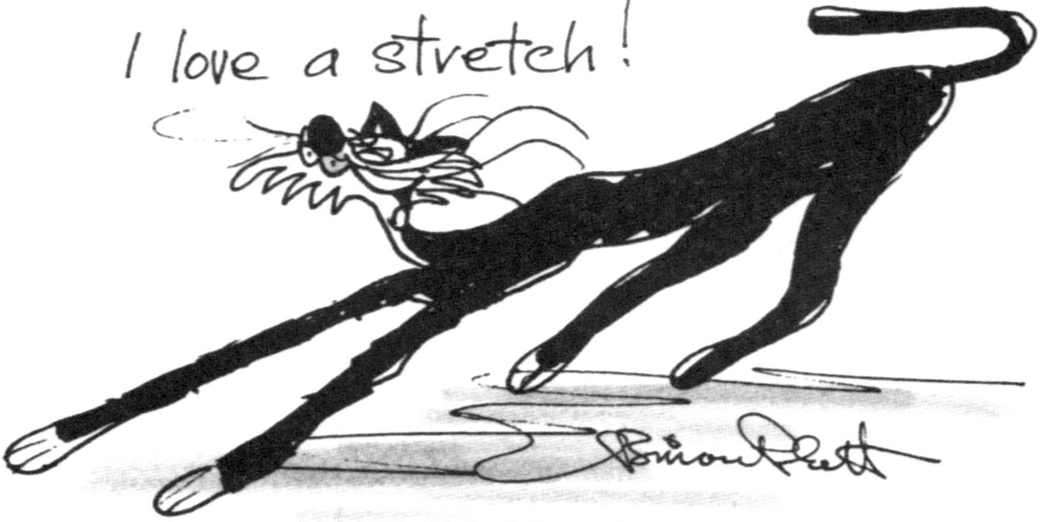
I love a stretch!

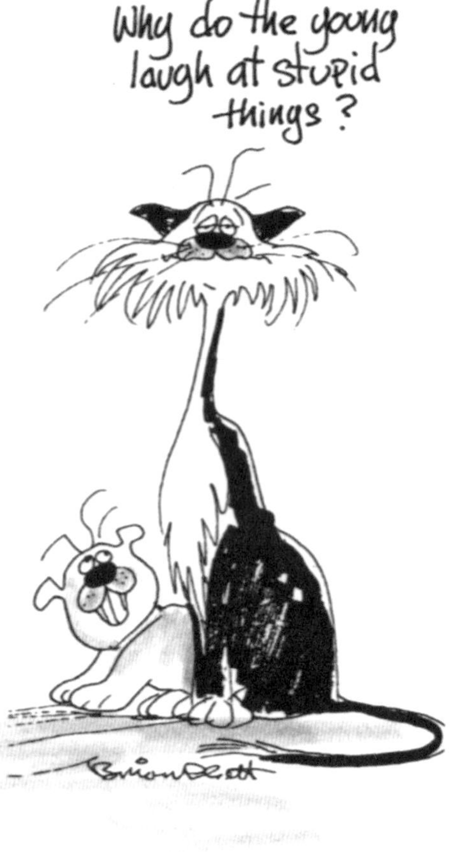
Why do the young laugh at stupid things?

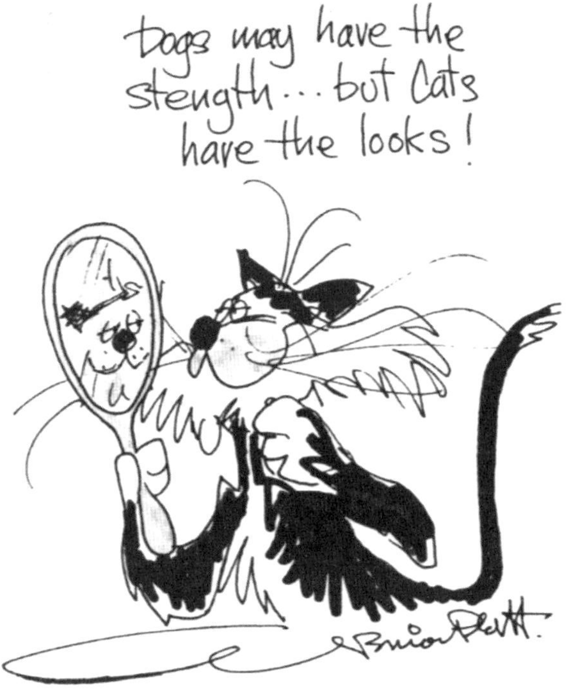
Dogs may have the stength... but Cats have the looks!
Brian Platt.

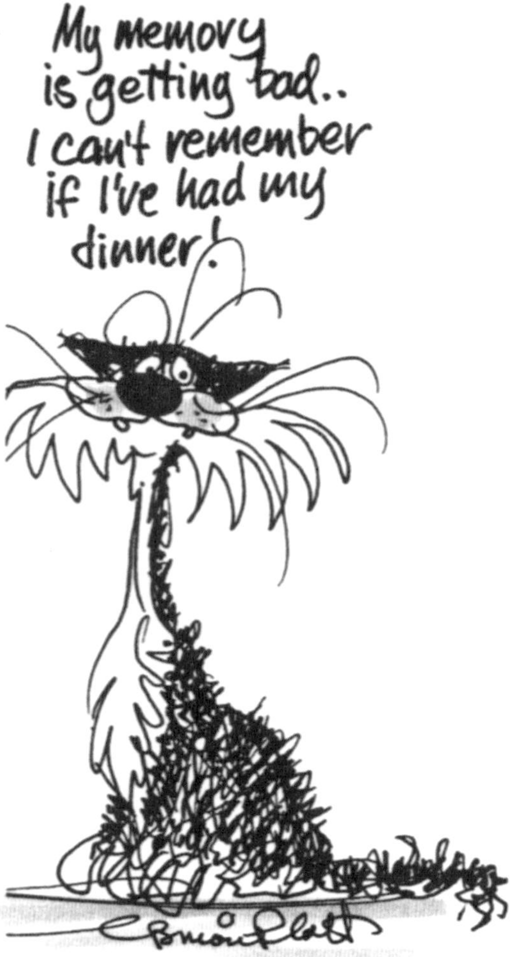
My memory is getting bad.. I can't remember if I've had my dinner!

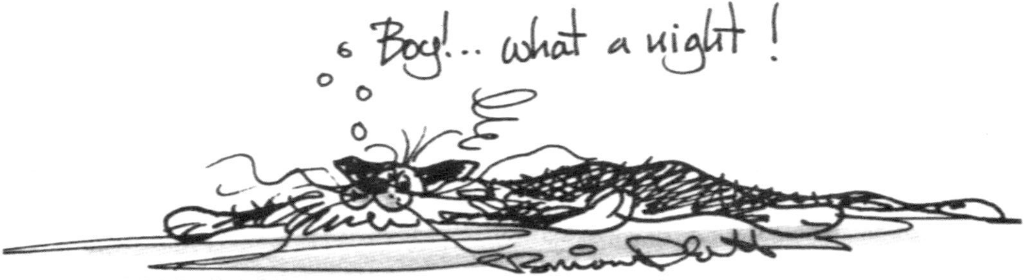
Bog!... what a night!

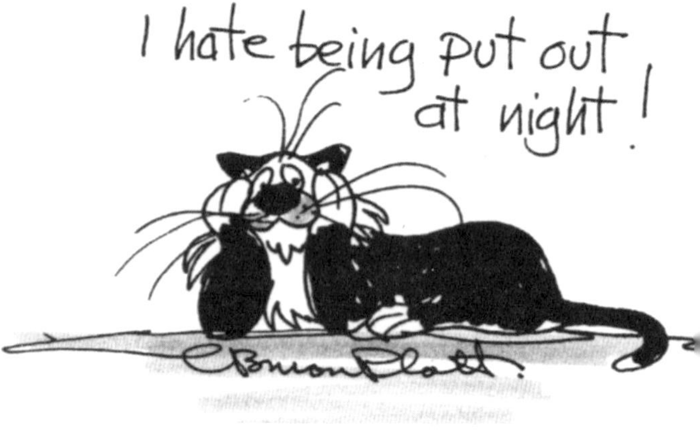
I hate being put out at night!

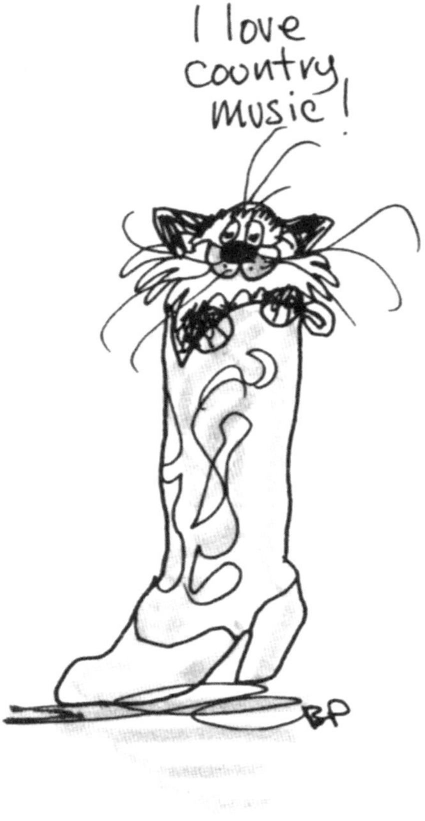
I love country music!
BP

there's more to life than being a smart cat!

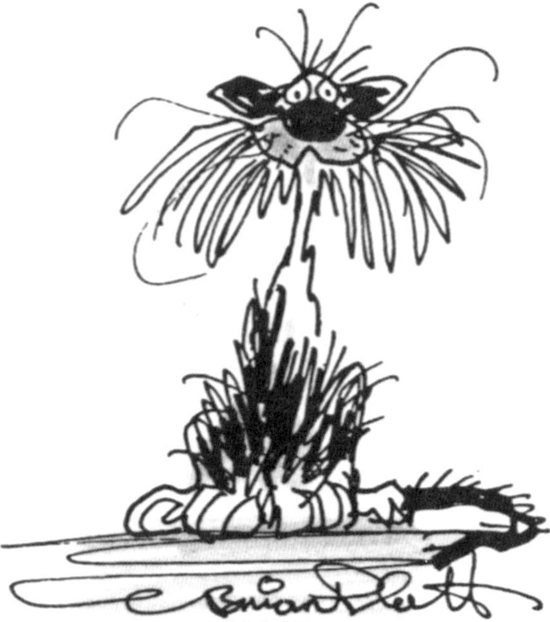

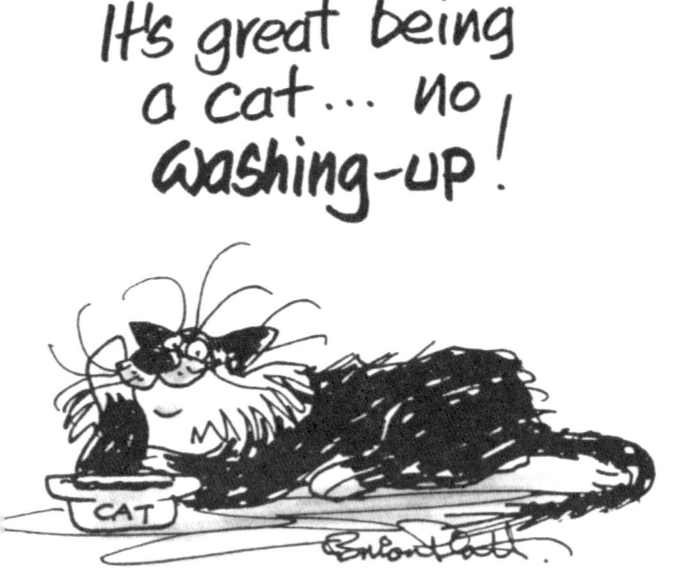
It's great being a cat... no washing-up!
CAT

All my life i've been Scruffy!

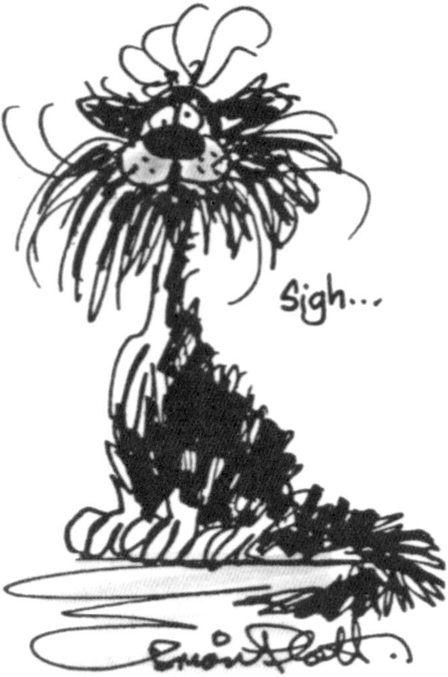
Sigh...

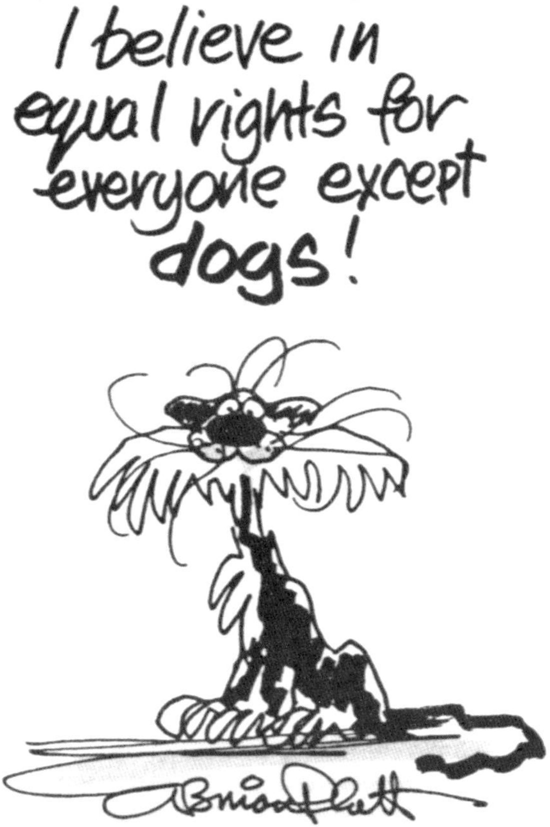
I believe in equal rights for everyone except dogs!

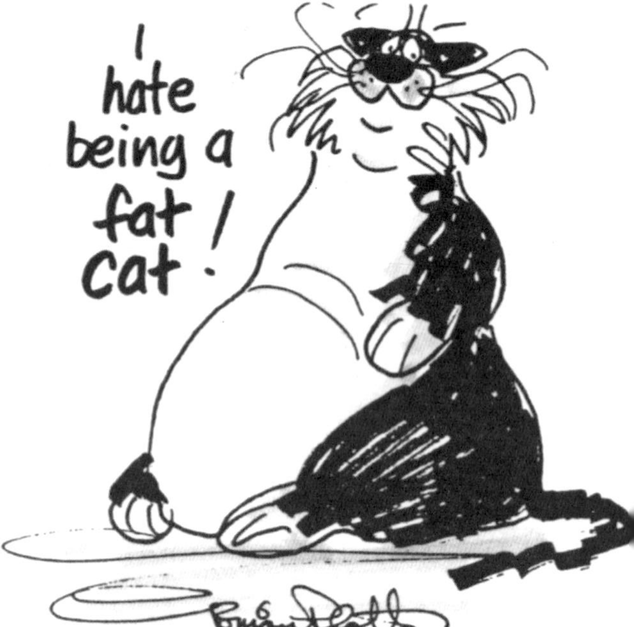
I hate being a fat cat!